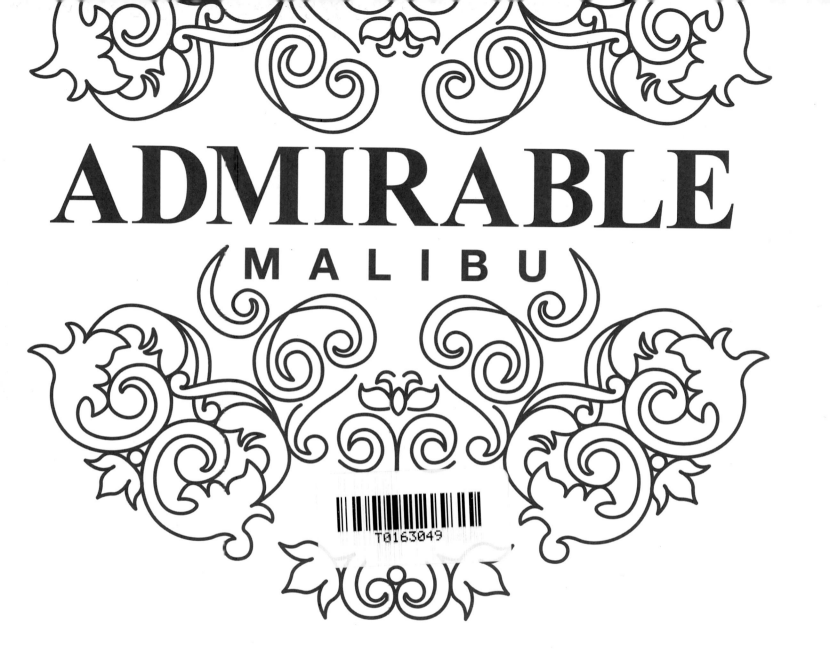

ADMIRABLE
MALIBU

T0163049

Admirable Family Vineyards
The Wine Roads of California

Wine-Inspired Coloring for Drinking Age Roamers

Tal Wiszniak-Shani

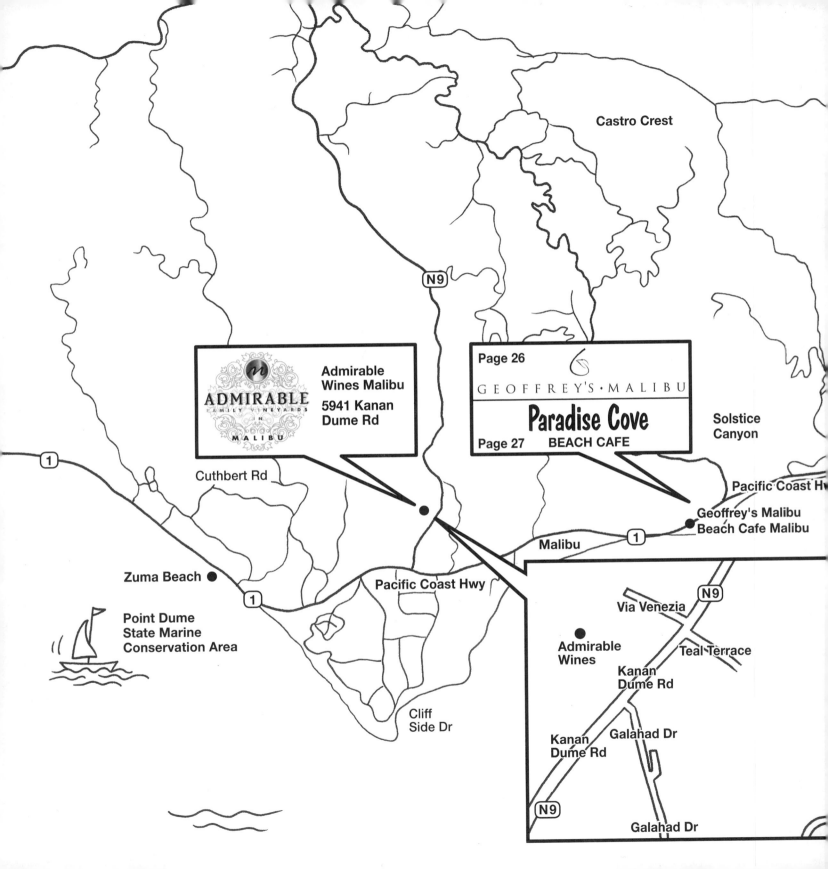

Castro Crest

N9

Admirable Wines Malibu

5941 Kanan Dume Rd

ADMIRABLE
FAMILY VINEYARDS
IN
MALIBU

Page 26

GEOFFREY'S · MALIBU

Paradise Cove

Page 27   BEACH CAFE

Solstice Canyon

Cuthbert Rd

Pacific Coast Hw

1

Geoffrey's Malibu
Beach Cafe Malibu

Malibu

1

N9

Via Venezia

Zuma Beach

Pacific Coast Hwy

Admirable
Wines

Teal Terrace

1

Point Dume
State Marine
Conservation Area

Kanan
Dume Rd

Galahad Dr

Cliff
Side Dr

Kanan
Dume Rd

N9

Galahad Dr

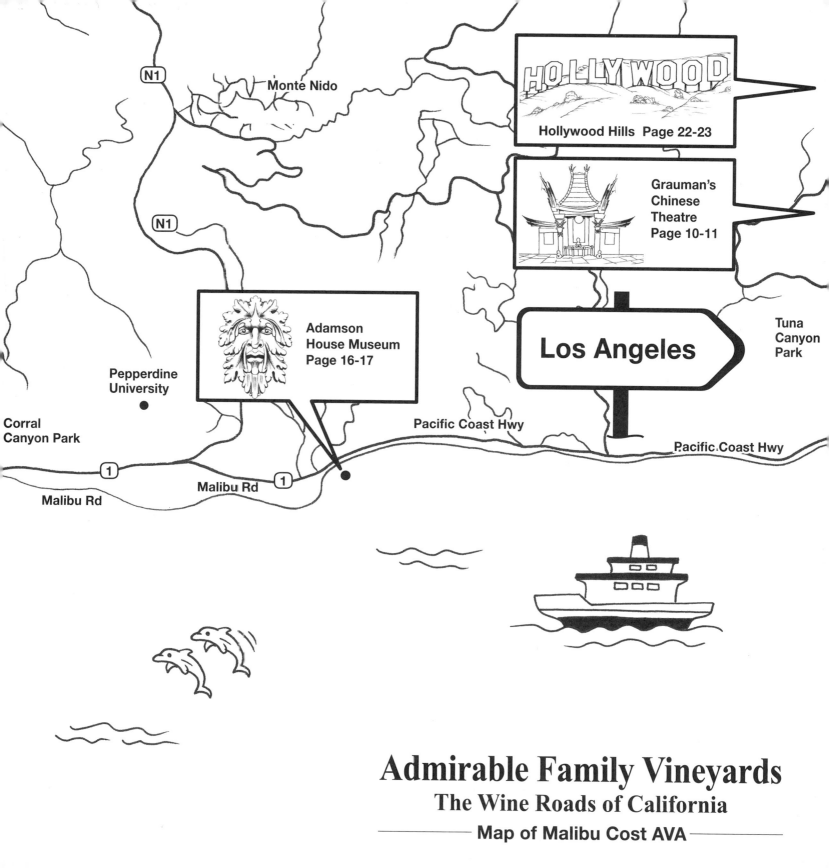

N1

Monte Nido

N1

Hollywood Hills Page 22-23

**Grauman's
Chinese
Theatre
Page 10-11**

Tuna
Canyon
Park

**Adamson
House Museum
Page 16-17**

Los Angeles

Pepperdine
University

Corral
Canyon Park

Pacific Coast Hwy

Pacific Coast Hwy

1

Malibu Rd   1

Malibu Rd

Admirable Family Vineyards
The Wine Roads of California
— Map of Malibu Cost AVA —

The Location

Throughout the year, Malibu vineyards benefit from abundant light reflected from the sea, and have perfect soil conditions for growing premium grapes. The nearby ocean ensures thermic breezes that cool the vines during the warm periods of the year. The coastal fog prevents dehydration of the plants, creating conditions more easily found at northern latitudes, facilitating long, slow, and continuous maturation of the grapes, favoring long-chain polyphenols, perfectly mature crunchy tannins, and an extremely rich aromatic balance.

Facing: A sculpture by famed artist **Nathalie Decoster** greets guests to Malibu Family Vineyards with its message of renewal.

The Vines

The wines produced from the Malibu slopes exude a delicate character with hints of mineral sea air. The acres of Viognier are planted on the slopes facing southwest, while the Syrah and Cabernet Sauvignon face southeast. Both vines benefit from the temperate maritime climate of the California coast. The sea breezes dry the vines after morning dew or rain and contribute to reducing the risks of disease. And the misty fog in both morning and night cools down the Californian heat and sun.

Admirable Family Vineyards

Malibu Pearl

Viognier 95%, Chardonnay 5%

Private Reserve 2015, Malibu Coast AVA

Grauman's Chinese Theatre at Hollywood and Highland

The iconic LA landmark opened May 18, 1927 with the premiere of Cecil B. DeMille's film The King of Kings. With its forecourt flooring of concrete impression of signatures and hand-and footprints of celebrities from the 20s to today, the scene is pure, old-Hollywood grandeur.

Frank Sinatra, whose handprints can be found right next to Julie Andrews', had this to say (or rather sing) about wine (and bad advice):

"Someone said drink the water, but I will drink the wine / Someone said take a poor man, the rich don't have a dime / Go fool yourself, if you will, I just haven't got the time / I'll give you back your water, and I will take the wine."

Admirable Family Vineyards

"It Takes Two"

Syrah 80%, Cabernet Sauvignon 20%

Private Reserve 2014
Malibu Coast AVA

Admirable Family Vineyards

Bord de l'Eau

Cabernet Sauvignon 73%, Merlot 10%,
Cabernet Franc 9%, Petit Verdot 8%

Historic Adamson House &
Malibu Lagoon Museum
23200 Pacific Coast Highway

The father of the builder of this California landmark, and the last owner of the Malibu Spanish Land Grant, called Malibu "The American Riviera." He wasn't referring to its suitability as a grape growing hub at the time, just an ideal place to build a family estate.

But the Provençal truth of it is in the tasting.

Just down the highway from Malibu Family Vineyards, it is a genuine Malibu gem and a must-see site.

Facing: An example of the striking ceramic art that can be found everywhere on the amazing Adamson House property.

Admirable Family Vineyards

So Happy!

Chardonnay 96%, Pinot Noir 4%

———— 2015 ————

California AVA

"Surf...

Admirable Family Vineyards

Fantastic 4

Cabernet-Sauvignon 45%, Cabernet-Franc 25%,
Merlot 20%, Syrah 10%

Which celebrity or celebrities don't own vineyards?

-Francis Ford Coppola
-Drew Barrymore
-Brad Pitt
-Harrison Ford

Admirable Family Vineyards

Blanc & Blanc

Viognier 98%, Chardonnay 2%

"*Heady Notes of Honeysuckle*"

**27400 Pacific Coast Hwy,
Malibu, CA 90265**

GEOFFREY'S · MALIBU

Admirable Family Vineyards

Vigneronne

"The Winemaker"

Syrah 56%, Merlot 43%

Board and Bench Publishing
Boardandbench.com

ISBN: 978-1-935879-97-8
Printed in Canada

Although all reasonable care has been taken in the preparation of this book, neither the illustrator/author nor the publisher can accept liability for any consequences arising from the information or the representations contained herein.